Kosovo War Poetry

Personal Note

The way human beings inflict horror and suffering upon themselves both fascinates and scares me. The tendency to violence is the flaw in human personality that maximises human misery and endangers the entire species. As such it deserves our serious and continuing attention.

Wars in Kosovo and Serbia, to which NATO nations contributed, demonstrate the havoc and wretchedness that our tendency to violence can cause and are matters that concern all responsible people.

My poems are simply a personal attempt to record and respond to the conflicts. Like most UK citizens I was involved daily throughout the war watching it on TV, listening to the radio and reading about it in the newspapers. I am involved as a tax payer, voter, and supporter (or otherwise) of a NATO government.

In some poems I set up other people's ideas for consideration. So that there may be no confusion I would like to state that I unreservedly condemn: 1) the systematic racial abuse, removal of human rights, arbitrary arrest, torture, destruction of homes and murder of Kosovo Albanians by Serbs over many years; 2) the violence of the KLA against Serbs; 3) the bombing of Yugoslavia by NATO; 4) the murder and violence against Serbs, Roma, and Gorani carried out by Kosovo Albanians from June 99 onwards. I would suggest that all the violence has served only to make situations worse.

I hope that the questions raised in my poetry and verse will provoke thought about violent conflicts and help, in a small way, to encourage the development of wiser international policy.

My thanks to John Bedford for proof reading the text in a very narrow time slot, and to the editors of *Day by Day* who were the first to publish four of the *Kosovo War Poems*.

David Roberts, 18 January 2000

Kosovo War Poetry and Verse

with background notes

David Roberts

Saxon Books

ISBN 0 9528969 2 3

First published 2000 by
Saxon Books 221 London Road Burgess Hill
West Sussex RH15 9RN UK
Phone/fax 01 444 232 356

Web sites: www.warpoetry.co.uk
and www.saxonbooks.co.uk

Printed and bound in Great Britain

Front cover painting by David Roberts. Back cover is a photograph taken by a Serb soldier in Kosovo and accidentally left behind. First published in *The Times*.

CONTENTS

Euro-tragedy 1999/2000

Poetry and Verse

Euro-tragedy 1999/2000

The war in Serbia and Kosovo - A tragedy doubled

Europeans witnessed an extraordinary, two-fold tragedy in 1999. A race-war conducted by the Serbs under President Milosevic drove hundreds of thousands of Kosovo Albanians from their homes, and NATO, the most powerful military alliance the world has ever known, conducted the most intensive bombing campaign in the history of warfare against Serbia, the poorest and most miserable country in Europe.

For eleven weeks the war dominated the media. Since then the immense tragedy and crime of the war have faded from public view. Yet the desperate human consequences, and the long-term costs remain. The moral and military principles which guided the NATO campaign go unchallenged and unexamined.

Starting on 24 March 1999 the war was a 78 day concerted action by the air forces of 13 of NATO's 19 member nations. It was the first time in the fifty years' existence of NATO that its forces had been used aggressively - in direct conflict with the terms of its own treaty which specifically recognises the United Nations as the principle organisation responsible for peace and security in the world.

By asserting at the outset that ground troops would not be used NATO leaders made possible, and likely, the escalation of Milosevic's race war against the Albanians in Kosovo. In the end 868,000 Kosovo Albanians, out of a total population of 1.8 million, fled their homes and their country - mainly into neighbouring Albania, Montenegro, and Macedonia.

In Kosovo, Serb soldiers damaged or destroyed in the region of 100,000 homes. Of these, 50,000 homes were totally destroyed. The numbers killed by the Serbs during the war are variously estimated at between a few hundred and a few thousand. By the first week of January 2000 one third of the 529 known mass graves had been opened and 2108 bodies had been discovered. Many of these will be Serbians either killed by NATO bombs or the Kosovo Liberation Army which fought the Serbians in Kosovo throughout the NATO air campaign. Five thousand Kosovo Albanians have been reported missing presumed dead. In addition there are believed to be between 3000 and 7000 Kosovars still held in Serb prisons. Understandably this fact causes intense anger.

The stated aim of the NATO bombing campaign was to put an end to the "ethnic cleansing" and return the Kosovo Albanian refugees to their homes. Whilst it is literally true to say that the objective was achieved the implied aim of quickly bringing an end to the suffering of the Albanians was not achieved. Worse still, the anguish of the Albanians was immediately hugely increased as a direct consequence of the NATO action. The physical state of Kosovo was dramatically damaged, the political situation became even less clear and satisfactory, and a "reverse ethnic cleansing" of Serbs and Roma by Albanians was precipitated.

Furthermore, the innocent Serbian civilian population was terrorised and their failing economy was ruined by a disproportionate bombing campaign that was almost irrelevant to combating the ongoing atrocities in Kosovo. The entire area of the Federal Republic of Yugoslavia is now, at the outset of the twenty-first century, one of immense human suffering and political uncertainty far worse than the situation before NATO flew in on its so-called humanitarian mission. The peaceful development of the region has been set back a generation.

The worsening of the tragedy might have been avoided. In the months and years before March 1999, more could have been done to deal with the grievances and aspirations of the Kosovo Albanians. Support might have been given to their claims for independence. International monitors working in Kosovo might have been reinforced. The negotiations in Rambouillet, near Paris, in early 1999, on the status of Kosovo might have been prolonged till agreement was reached. Instead, NATO demanded that Kosovo should be allowed a referendum on total independence and insisted that NATO forces should occupy both Kosovo *and* Serbia. It was impossible for Milosevic to sign such an outrageous document. Interestingly, NATO, in its desperation to end the war, agreed to drop two of these demands.

Serbia's suffering before 24 March

The leadership of Milosevic was calamitous. Within the space of a few years, as a direct result of his promotion of Serbian nationalism and racism, the old Yugoslavia disintegrated. Conflicts with the former republics of Yugoslavia were fostered and costly wars, the destruction of ancient cities, the deliberate inflaming of racist hatred, appalling massacres and the displacement of thousands of people from their homes within the former Yugoslavia had followed inevitably from Milosevic's policies. One by one the republics declared independence. The economy of Serbia, which was already in difficulty, suffered further when the United Nations imposed sanctions.

Countless intellectuals and professionals fled abroad to lead a better life. Those that stayed in Serbia experienced raging inflation, worsening living conditions, and in a population of 11 million there were 400,000 unemployed.

Serbia was also the victim of "ethnic cleansing" as well as a perpetrator. At the start of 1999 there were 500,000 Serbian refugees in Serbia purged from Croatia (with the backing of the United States) and from Bosnia.

The effects of the bombing of Serbia

In eleven weeks the NATO air forces flew over 36,000 sorties and dropped over 23,000 bombs and missiles on the Federal Republic of Yugoslavia (Serbia, Vojvodina, Kosovo, and Montenegro). These included 400 cruise missiles, cluster bombs, and highly toxic depleted uranium bombs.

Targets included the military forces, bases and equipment of the Serbian army. In addition the bombing damaged or destroyed 144 major industrial plants including all Yugoslavia's oil refineries, fuel storage facilities, car and motorcycle factories, pharmaceutical and fertiliser factories, rubber factories. The bombing of some of these released large quantities of dangerous chemicals into the environment, created an oil slick on the Danube 20 kilometres long, and put 600, 000 people out of work.

Damaged or destroyed were several thousand homes (mainly in Belgrade, Nis, Cuprija, Aleksinac and Pristina), 33 clinics and hospitals, 340 schools, 55 road and rail bridges. The River Danube was blocked; some of the bridges were hundreds of miles from the scenes of the racial expulsions and were vital trade links to the rest of Europe. Also attacked were 12 railway lines, 5 civilian airports, 6 trunk roads, 10 TV and radio stations and 24 transmitters; power stations were put out of action; sewage treatment plants were damaged; water supplies were cut off.

Five thousand civilians were injured; 1400 adult civilians were killed, 600 children were killed, 600 military and police personnel were killed. As a result of the murder, harassment, violence, and destruction of homes carried out by the returning Kosovo Albanians there are now about 150,000 further refugees (mainly Serbs and Roma) in Serbia who have fled from Kosovo. "Ethnic cleansing" has not been halted. There are now 10,000 unexploded bombs scattered throughout the Federal Republic of Yugoslavia. Serbia is now the most polluted, damaged, distressed, politically unsettled, and poverty-stricken country in Europe. It is an humanitarian disaster area and has the highest UNHCR[1] budget of any country in the world.

The old Yugoslavia

In the 1980's Yugoslavia lived in relative peace. It was a popular holiday destination for millions of European tourists. They went to enjoy the warm hospitality, the Adriatic sea and beaches, and the wonderful summer climate. At this time Yugoslavia consisted of

[1] UNHCR - the United Nations refugee relief organisation

the six republics of Slovenia, Croatia, Bosnia-Herzegovina, Montenegro, Macedonia and Serbia. Serbia contained two self-governing regions - Vojvodina bordering Hungary and Romania in the north, and Kosovo bordering Albania and Macedonia in the south. Within the six republics were five main ethnic groups, four languages, three religions and two alphabets.

Kosovo's years of suffering

In 1968 demonstrators in Kosovo had demanded that it should be recognised as a separate republic. In 1969 the Albanian language University of Pristina was established. In 1974 Kosovo became a self-governing region within the Federal Republic of Yugoslavia.

During the 70's and 80's the Albanian population within Kosovo increased and the Serbian population of that area declined - partly because of a lower Serbian birth rate, partly because of an exodus of Serbians from the area. Some Serbians claim to have been harassed by Albanians. By 1999 Albanians were 90 per cent of the population of Kosovo.

On 11 March 1981 students at Pristina University demonstrated against the food and conditions there. Crowds swelled the demonstrations; many people were arrested.

Two weeks later more demonstrations followed with workers joining students in six towns in Kosovo. Protesters called for Kosovo to be made an independent republic. Extra police were drafted in from Serbia and tanks appeared in the streets. More than 2000 demonstrators were arrested. Prison sentences varied from one month to fifteen years. Amnesty International records that over 300 people were killed in protests in Kosovo in 1981.

Out of a population at that time of 1.5 million only 178,000 had jobs - and a disproportionate number of these went to Serbs and Montenegrins. Both Serbs and Albanians blamed each other for their problems and racist/nationalist abuse began to be promoted in books and the press. Media power was on the side of the Serbians who produced an avalanche of racist anti-Albanian material. Serbs made unjustifiable allegations of rape, intimidation and murder against the Albanians in Kosovo.

In 1988 Milosevic had decided to reduce the powers and independence of the Kosovo Albanians and removed two local leaders from the assembly in Pristina - Azem Vlassi and Kacqusha Jashari. Huge demonstrations with in excess of 100,000 people erupted in support of the leaders.

In 1989 the Serbian Assembly began to remove the independence of Kosovo and gave control of Kosovo's police, courts, civil defence, social, economic and education policy, and choice of official language, to Belgrade. This meant that teaching in the Albanian language was effectively suspended.

Further huge demonstrations occurred throughout Kosovo; the Serbians sent in more troops and tanks, and a state of emergency was declared. Hundreds of protesters were arrested and jailed.

In March the provincial assembly of Kosovo (infiltrated by Serbians) met and voted through constitutional amendments yielding power to Belgrade. Once again there were huge demonstrations. Thousands of workers, administrators and intellectuals were arrested and some were kept in solitary confinement for months without access to defence lawyers. Between 1981 and 1989 584,373 arrests took place - about half the adult population.

In June 1990 the authorities closed down the Albanian language newspaper, *Rilindja*; closed the Kosovo Academy of Arts and Science, and dismissed thousands of state employees.

In July the Kosovo assembly tried to enact new measures against the Albanians, but when it became clear that members were not going to co-operate with the leaders the assembly was adjourned and members were locked out. The excluded members met in the street outside the locked assembly building and declared Kosovo "independent within Yugoslavia." The Serbian assembly in Belgrade reacted by dissolving the Kosovo assembly.

In October 1991 both Slovenia and Croatia declared themselves independent. In 1992 Bosnia-Herzegovina and Macedonia did the same. What remained of the former Yugoslavia is known as the Federal Republic of Yugoslavia and consists of Serbia (with its seat of government in Belgrade) and the constituent provinces of Vojvodina and Kosovo, plus Montenegro.

On 24 May 1992 Albanians in Kosovo ran their own elections (declared illegal by Serbia) for their independent republican assembly. Ibrahim Rugova was elected President of the "Republic of Kosovo" and his party, the Democratic League of Kosovo (LDK) became the ruling party. The policy of the new republic was a) to be pacifist in its methods, being opposed to violent revolution; b) to deny Serbia's claimed rights to govern Kosovo; c) to seek international support for diplomatic mediation and UN involvement in the running of Kosovo. Some gestures of support were made by the "international community" but Kosovo's independence was not recognised.

As protests continued the response of the Serbian authorities in Kosovo was to sack everyone involved in demonstrations. In this way 6,000 teachers lost their jobs. The remaining teachers were sacked when they refused to comply with a new curriculum which virtually eliminated Albanian literature and history. Most Albanian doctors and health workers were dismissed. As a matter of necessity the Albanian population set up alternative, parallel systems of education and health care, funding them with a voluntary 3 per cent tax.

Arbitrary arrest of Albanians in Kosovo became the norm. There were 15,000 such arrests in 1994. Many were tortured. Homes were frequently raided by the police and property and money stolen by them. In 1994 there were 3,500 such raids.

Albanian pacifism ends

The restraint exercised by the Albanian population in the face of sustained abuses of their basic human rights was admirable and remarkable. Unfortunately Rugova's non-violent approach did not end the Serbian abuse of the Albanian majority in Kosovo or attract international support, and in 1996 young men lost patience with his policy. Armed attacks and murders of Serbians began and an organisation calling itself the Kosovo Liberation Army (KLA) claimed responsibility. Attacks increased in the next three years as did revenge attacks by the Serbs. In response to revenge attacks many more young men were attracted to the KLA. From now on the international community would have to take the plight of the Albanians in Kosovo very much more seriously. - See *The Path to War*, page 37.

By March of 1998 the conflict had become a full scale war. The Serbian army was shelling Albanian villages in the Drenica Valley. The KLA attacked Serbian forces. See *Kosovo: Prelude to War*, page 19. By July the KLA claimed to have control of one third of Kosovo.

In September the UN Security Council called for a cease-fire and warned of the possibility of taking "additional measures". Milosevic agreed to withdraw troops, but failed to carry this out.

In October NATO made its momentous mistake: it threatened military action if Milosevic did not agree to unacceptable terms. (See pages 8 and 9.) Milosevic refused, and called NATO's bluff.

NATO's miscalculations

By 24 March 1999 100,000 Kosovo Albanians had already left the country. They had been terrified by threats, killings, and the looting and burning of homes by Serbian soldiers. NATO failed to calculate that by announcing that it would not deploy ground forces Milosevic would feel free to increase the pace of the expulsion of Albanians. The refugee problem alone was increased ten fold by NATO's action - first by this increased rate of expulsion and second by the expulsion of Serbs, Roma and Gorani which occurred when the Albanians returned. The refugee crisis created by the returning Albanians is now far greater than the one which existed when NATO first took military action in March 1999.

NATO's targeting was not focused exclusively on the military enemy. In fact it became ever more widespread and desperate. No reasonable person could accept that the targeting of civilian infrastructure was anything other than a war against the innocent Serbian civilian population. It brought not peace to Serbia, but death, destruction and misery. The war which NATO leaders claimed was humanitarian used the most advanced military technology to achieve a result that was simply barbaric, a crime against humanity.

Why the war ended

The war ended when Milosevic agreed to withdraw his troops from Kosovo on the understanding that Kosovo would remain part of the Federal Republic of Yugoslavia, and that NATO forces would not enter Serbia. The terms that settled the war, if they had been offered at Rambouillet, might have prevented the disaster. Milosevic's forces had not run out of fuel, weapons, ammunition, or men. Undoubtedly the suffering endured by Serbian civilians could not be sustained indefinitely. But the move which prompted Milosevic to act was the withdrawal of support by the one remaining country that sided with Serbia: Russia. The motivation of Russia was not admirable. Russia was bribed. The International Monetary Fund agreed to write off £3 billion interest payment on its foreign debt. It would seem that the more assiduous fostering of Russian support at an earlier stage of the conflict might have prevented much suffering, but paying for support set a very bad precedent. In international law no military action should have been taken without the backing of the United Nations. The harm done to relations with Russia could have been avoided.

The Kosovo problem, January 2000

Peace has emphatically not returned to Kosovo. The political situation there is more confused and uncertain than it ever was before. There are now four forces claiming the right to rule.

NATO countries agreed that Kosovo would remain part of the Federal Republic of Yugoslavia. Serbia therefore expects to be consulted on the running of the country, but is effectively ignored. The elected Democratic League of Kosovo is also sidelined.

The returning KLA which is now officially disbanded as a military force, and is not elected, took immediate control of the running of the country from early June 1999. Hacim Thaci, who was the leader of the KLA, is the popular though unelected self-proclaimed Prime Minister of the "Provisional Government of Kosovo." The UN-backed KFOR military force with 45,000 troops and 3000 police drawn from 44 countries regards itself as the keeper of the peace and the organiser of the state. It is valiantly struggling to establish justice, peace, and democracy.

In addition there are over 300 non-governmental and governmental organisations dealing with housing, food, and other basic necessities and offering counselling and comfort.

As first steps towards a long-term solution of the problem gangster morality must end: the Kosovo Albanians must understand that their abuse of Serbians is unacceptable, just as the abuse of Kosovo Albanians by Serbians was unacceptable; a form of government agreeable to Kosovo Albanians must be found. It is very regrettable that NATO, in its haste to end the war, made an agreement with Milosevic which anybody might reasonably have guessed would infuriate Kosovo Albanians. NATO will need to renegotiate. The suffering of the Serb people must be recognised and help provided.

Great wrongs have been done. America and the nations of Europe need each other's forgiveness. - The tragedy continues.

War Spectacular

And here is Kate Adie.

Behind me on this warship you can see
primed for targets two hundred miles distant
the first cruise missiles
to be launched in this campaign.

With a thunderous roar, and right on cue,
the million dollar rockets rise into the night
then arch and head east.

Such fireworks leave us all impressed.

And here we have the refugees, the dispossessed,
a pitiful procession of bewildered humanity,
thousands of them in endless convoy
fleeing from the Serbian terror.
They tell of identity papers
snatched from them by troops at the border
of their homes now looted and torched.
We see, close up, their haunted eyes.
We are moved by the human face of suffering.

And now for the rest of tonight's news.

3 December 99

Kate Adie is the BBC Chief News Correspondent. She was with the US Sixth Fleet in the Adriatic for the start of the war and reported the launch of the cruise missiles from a US warship.

Tempting War

The nature of war is different now.
When the Western Federation flies in
only the losing nation suffers losses,
and the Federation will always win.

8 July 99

Centre of Learning

Does anyone really know what the effects are of
1 racism?
2 race wars?
3 ethnic cleansing?
4 repression of minorities?
5 repression of majorities?
6 removal of human rights?
7 militarism?
8 fettered media?
9 police corruption?
10 political assassinations?
11 a gangster economy?
12 a culture of revenge?

Study in the Balkans.
Long-term practical experiment in progress.

11 July 99

Kosovo: Prelude to War

On the edge of Europe
a green valley
is quiet in the summer heat
far from the stress and noise
of civilisation.
Who would not love
to live
in a place like this?

Down in the valley
just audible
a sheep bleats
fire crackles
and smoke drifts slowly
from burning houses.

Along the valley
hundreds of Albanian homes
burn.

It is the Serbs.
It is the Serbs.
Their troops and police . . .
They have come with tanks . . .

Six men with picks and spades
dig six deep graves
in the stony earth.
A group of men watch the grim work.

A passing cyclist gives a sideways look.

A burnt out house.
Two men watch through the glassless window.
More stand outside, waiting.

Inside,
men, with white handkerchiefs
tied round their faces,
and wearing red rubber gloves
examine the black ash
and the charred remains
of missing men.

I know this buckle from a belt.
This is Rahim.

This body, smaller
must be Ismet.
He was sixteen.
The youngest.

Eight men are missing.
A man turns over the blackened metal
of a pocket knife.

This body is my brother.

The body is burnt meat on bones.
Charred black -
a frame inconveniently sprawled.

Several men
have joined the searchers.

They stand like a half circle of statues.
Impassively they watch.

An outsize sheet of polythene lines a coffin.
Two men easily lift in the blackened form.
Crisp black ash crumbles and rattles
as they re-pose the limbs.
They fold over the sheeting.

Six coffins are filled.

Allah is great!
Allah is great!
O creator of the universe!
We gather here to express our sorrow.
Not to question your will
but to express our anger
at the injustice and terror
inflicted on our people.
The blood
shed by our sons and daughters
will serve to strengthen our roots
in our ancient homeland.
They will never be forgotten.

Hundreds are gathered in a seething tide.
The coffins are born shoulder high.
Close behind, a line of women
with white head scarves,
stunned with grief,
walk shoulder to shoulder.
The people - a close gathered unity -

flow across the hillside
to the prepared graves.

While many with spades
throw soil in the deep graves
tears stream
down distraught faces.
The stunned stand
in bewildered silence.

But Serbs have villages too.
And the KLA have guns.

Quiet watchers -
young men, older men, two girls -
in a universal uniform of camouflage
in a hill top look-out
observe
the village in the valley.

It is a strange village:
through binoculars they see
no women,
no children,
men moving quickly,
all armed.
No hay has been cut.
No cattle graze.

And dead cattle,
rotting,
are strewn across a field.

It is a Serbian village
amongst Albanian villages.
Ethnically pure
and ethnically besieged.
Machine gun posts
manned day and night
defend the village,
the last Serbian village in this valley
to resist Albanian violence.
This is a last stand.

This is sacred Serbian land.
We have lived here
for a thousand years.
The whole village
would rather die
than let Albanians take it.
When we are all dead
they can have our village.
Really, we know we cannot win.

This is Albanian land.
We have lived here
since time began.
Why should the Serb
rule over us?
We are fighting
for our freedom.

The Serbs are vicious.
No-one is safe.
The Serb destroys
our animals
our crops
our homes
our wives
our children.
The Serbs have tanks.
One cop is killed
and they destroy a whole village.
Where will it end?
We haven't enough weapons
to win this war.
Why should we suffer?
What can we do?

Who would not want revenge?
But who cannot see
the futility of revenge?

This is a Serbian convent.
We are surrounded by Albanians.
They steal from us
and harass us.
They say we are on their territory.
But the convent has been here
for 500 years.
We are Christians.
We have vowed to God
that we'll never abandon the convent.
We'll stay here until death.

We worship war.
We celebrate war in our ancient songs.
"Men who fear war
are traitors.
Real men
die like martyrs.
Their lives
they gladly give,
So that
our country may live."

The trouble goes back to 1912.
The great powers
gave Kosovo to the Serbs.

This goes back to 1389.
The Turks fought us.
They were Muslims.
We are Christians.

We have lived here for 500 years.

We have lived here for 1000 years.

We have lived here since time began.

We are Albanians.

We are Serbs.

This is our land.
We live here.

We have always lived here.
We have nowhere else.
We live here.
This is our land.
And this is where we'll die.

Serbian troops
walked into a trap,
when they went to defend
Serbian villagers
under attack.

Another funeral.

Now there is noise of great distress.
A crowd is gathered
on the edge of a village.
There is helpless sobbing and moaning.

Four men
lift the first coffin,
covered in red, white and blue,
into a truck.
Distraught women
clamber round it.
One strokes the lid.
The father
with face like stone
stares at the coffin
transfixed.
The brother
his eyes red with tears

climbs into the truck
and rests his head on the coffin.

A military band plays dismal music.
The father stares at the coffin.
He stares, uncomprehending.
He stares at the coffin.

The slow beat of the drum.
The mournful brass of the band.
Men with faces of stone.
The slow procession moves off.
The howling and sobbing increase.
Grief without restraint.
Distress beyond belief.
Men with faces of stone.
The beat of the drum.
The cross carried at the front.
The procession moves swiftly.
Women carrying bouquets,
unseeing through their tears.
The mournful band.
The howling and crying.
Soldiers in grey,
their faces expressionless.
The crowds streaming after,
crossing the hillside
to
the waiting grave.

There is moaning and sobbing.
A convulsive scream
as soldiers carry the coffin forwards.
More soldiers stand in line,
faces without expression,
steeled against the emotion

that presses around them.
Soldiers in line
with guns at the ready.

The drum beats.
The band plays.
Faces blind with tears.
Faces of stone.
Sobbing and howling.
Grief without restraint.
The coffin is lowered.
The guns salute.
Three times they fire.
The red earth
is shovelled in.

That was my son.
He had a wife and four children.
He worked hard.
He was a good man.
Albanians were our neighbours.
I have liked them,
helped them all my life.
Who killed my son?
What madness came over them?
Why have we come to this?
Why can't we live together?
Why are we so blind?
We should stay as we were -
Christians, Muslims,
Albanians, Turks,
Gypsies and Serbs.
My father lived here

and my grandfathers.
Thirteen centuries we have lived here.
Why are we destroying everything we love?
We're helpless.
We're losing everything.
Nothing could be worse.

The fat cats in Belgrade
don't care about Kosovo.
This is no way to run a country.
We've been betrayed.
We're all victims now.

The valley burns.

There are people
with heavy burdens,
walking.

3-26 June 99

The ideas for this poem, came from a brilliant documentary film shown on UK Channel 4 TV. The film was called *The Valley*. It was produced and directed by Dan Read.

Do Not Doubt

Do not doubt these people.
This is a people's war.
They are united with their land
and will not move.
Their courage is beyond question.
They have suffered
but will not yield.
Their loyalty to each other
is absolute.
They are formidable people.
No force will ever move them
except death.

3 June 99

Time Divides and Destroys

They are living in the past
and dying in the present.
With a passion
they are loyal to the truth
of their sacred past.

Who are these people?
What is their sacred past?
Some say
they have lived here for a thousand years.

What!
No-one has lived here for a thousand years.

They are all new arrivals,
all temporary residents
with little time
to make the best
or the worst of
their one short life.
They are equal.

Yet they are loyal
to ideas that divide and destroy.

Divisions create fear.
Divisions create anger, hatred and violence.
Divisions make them suffer.
Divisions destroy their humanity.

Their commitment to the past
destroys their present.

So what hope for the future?

3 June and 1 September 99

Hatred

Both sides
have every reason
to hate and to fight.
Have not members of their families
been kidnapped?
Young men beaten?
Women and girls raped?
Crops destroyed?
Animals shot?
Homes torched?
Have not members of their families
been killed?

No one feels safe.

The situation is desperate.
They have suffered a reign of terror.
Their minds are in torment.
Whole communities
are traumatised.

No man
can tolerate
the destruction of his home
the murder of his children, his wife.
It seems that the destroyer must be destroyed.

What other way
can there be?

3 June and 1 September 99

Had a Nice Day

Yes, I've 'ad a nice day.
Me and Ivan set fire
to seven 'ouses.
Quite a blaze,
and a nice collection of souvenirs.

This afternoon we was layin' mines.

And 'ow are you, darlin' ?
And the kids?
Ah! Great!

Well, I'll 'ave to be goin' now.
Miss you darlin'.
Love ya!
Speak to ya soon.
Sweet dreams. Sweet dreams.

31 December 99

The Return

Agim from the KLA arrived.
Safe to return to the village, he said.

The villagers who had stayed high in the hills
knew what to expect.
They talked mostly of other things as they walked
slowly along stony paths, descending.

Hashim was with them. And not with them.

On the edge of the quiet group.
His thoughts were for his son.
He said nothing.

A haze of heat shimmered on burning stones.
Fierce light burned down upon the peasant group
descending through the trees,
through orchards, past fields of waiting corn.

Flies buzzed on fallen fruit.
From time to time the neighbours stopped.

They could see the village below them
at some distance:
a collection of blackened ruins,
ghostly in the glare of day.

Hashim recalled
how he had tried to restrain hot-head neighbours
who had set out to kill Serbs.
Angry, they would not listen.
They would not listen.

He was the last to enter the village.
Others, ahead were entering ruins
keen to know the worst.
Their voices rang out.

Here!
This is Halim.

This is Halim, look.
They shot him.
He fell in the fire.

This must be Ismet.

You know he had six children.
Did they escape?
Where is their mother?

We haven't found her.

Here is poor Rahim.
He was seventy. Such a kind man!

We'll start digging graves
for the fifteen we've found so far.

Hashim's question was not answered.

In the next house
he looked in
his friend Fehmi stood
staring at charred remains.
He was speechless.
Hashim, too. What could he say?

Beyond the village
a grassy track led into a wood.
Here were more bodies, fallen headlong,
smelling in the noonday heat,
flies busy on ghastly faces.

And here was his answer:
his son.

Poor Azem. My poor Azem.

So much,
for good intentions.

24 July, 15 September, 13 November 99

Bereft

Draw near.
Observe how his dignity impresses,
those everlasting clothes, shapeless, worn.
Peasant of ages, standing still,
craggy, stoic, grim,
unblinking, impassive.
Is this the way to mourn?

Is he really coping with the shock?
He seems hard, impervious, like a rock.

But may something be bruised and bleed within?

There are questions I would like to ask.
Does it still beat - his constricted heart?
Does brain still think? Do eyes still see?
Within his veins does blood still run?

He's quietly lost behind his mask,
and mercifully numb.

13 - 15 November 99

The Path to War

There is no justice
and voices of complaint are not heard
so there is hatred.
As there is hatred there is violence.
As there is violence there is retribution.
There is anger and greater anger
and a desire to destroy the causes of suffering.
So there is killing.
And retaliation.
And more killing.
Then you may call it war.

3 June 99

Come, NATO Bombs

Come, NATO bombs and fall on Serbs.
Deliver us from the fear of murder,
sudden arrests, mass imprisonments,
the fear of police abuse and torture.

Rain down. Rain down, NATO bombs.
May your guidance systems seek out Serbs.

Give us justice under the law.
Give us back our freedoms, our government,
newspapers, doctors, and teachers.
Give us freedom from press lies, hatred, racist attacks.

Rain down. Rain down, NATO bombs.
Cleanse our country of the Serbs.

So we prayed, and so the bombers came.
With deafening explosions
buildings, roads, bridges, military vehicles
were all blown away.

Night after night came terror from the skies -
enraging the Serbs who poured ever more soldiers into the country
carrying out mass executions, burning our homes,
renewing and escalating their savagery against us.

Drop more bombs, NATO, faster and faster.
Drive our Serb oppressors from our country.

So we prayed, and so they came -
more bombs,
more Serbs,
more terror.

And so we fled, loading our possessions,
children, old folk on trailers, on tractors,
abandoning our homes and our country,
fleeing in blind despair for the border.

We became a Biblical procession
an endless column of dazed humanity
trying to escape from the horror
of the twentieth century.

Could things ever be worse?
Things could be worse.

15 April 1999. NATO ADMITS BOMBING REFUGEES.
A NATO spokesman, Jamie Shea, said the pilot concerned had dropped the bomb in the belief that he was attacking a military convoy.
The alliance deeply regretted the loss of life.

1 November 99

The Worst That Could Happen

Kosovo in the chill of nightfall.
In the heart of Kosovo.
Mountains. Dark Forests. Last glimmers of light.

And dimly seen, a sight beyond belief:
a great lake, drained,
still moist, and glinting like an open wound,
black, but stained
with the blood of slaughtered dead -
bodies hurled in, thickly packed,
a sea floor of drowned,
as if the world itself were wrecked.

And round the margins of this great grave
where all their men have gone
numberless women of Kosovo weep.
Amongst them are the mothers
of those who ordered
many men here to be murdered.

All scan the nameless tumbled masses.
Tears blur and sight confuses.
Tantalised by hope, all hope - but they know
all hope must die. These are the missing.
Together, as in a trance, they grieve.
Together they stand,
stunned by the slow pains of grief.

Poor women of Kosovo,
what happy futures had you planned?
And your children, were they full of hope?
Now into this great void you stare.
The night is dark, and black the stars.
You are cold like ice, in this darkest night.
Tears shine on cheeks, such pitiful light.

What horrors have these women witnessed? -
Woken from sleep, their homes surrounded.
The doors broken in by masked men with guns.
Their men defenceless; how could they protect?
Ordered at gun-point into the street.

Young men, old men and boys, defenceless.
"You disease-carrying vermin must die.
You carry a virus, an alien ethnicity."

They were herded like plague-carrying cattle,
loaded in lorries, taken off in the night.

The women listened. With cold fear they shook.
Then in the distance, for a long time they heard it:

the sound of machine guns

mowing men down in a harvest of blood.

Later the carcasses,
bulldozed in pits.

Women of Kosovo,
you have cried beyond tears.
You have suffered heart-ache beyond aching.
Your hearts are broken beyond breaking.

Here is the heart of Kosovo.
This is the heart. The black heart
of Kosovo. Broken. Dark.

The worst that could happen,
has been done.

17 July - 19 August 99

The Accountants of Kosovo

The accountants of Kosovo
study the figures,
calculating costs.
Serbian dead: Albanian dead.

Serious losses again this year.
The books never balance.

There is never a profit.

We must seek clarification
of corporate objectives,
but how can we
when there are no directors?

Our task is baffling
We can only report
that we are at a loss.

There is no profit.

There is no prophet.

28 July 99

NATO Leaders

NATO's Christian leaders
had to respond to "irresistible fact."
"The time for doing nothing is over,"
they said. "It's time now for us to act."

"Destruction of property and lives by Serbians
has shocked us to the core.
We'll smash Serbia senseless
to teach Serbian soldiers not to make war.

We won't say this to the media
because bombing people is obscene.
We'll say we'll only target
the Serbian military machine.

To Serb soldiers sweeping through Kosovo,
looting, killing, and wrecking the place,
we offer just one major piece of encouragement:
our ground troops you won't have to face.

Our aim is to protect and to save lives.
We'll do our best to minimise distress.
We have the power to act for humanity,
and our missiles and bombs are the best."

7 July and 11 December 99

NATO Bombers

We are NATO bombers.
We fly high in the sky.
We fire laser-guided missiles
and we never ever die.

We are Christian bombers
aiming to break the Serbian will
by destroying most of Serbia
whilst trying not to kill.

From this moral high point
We drop our bombs with care.
Please disregard the outcome:
our motives make it fair.

The Serbian killing is evil
and their choice of victims deliberate:
NATO's bombing is to save lives
and the deaths we cause are indiscriminate.

We are NATO bombers;
our motives are the best:
we bomb the innocent Serbians
to influence the rest.

We are logical thinkers.
We bear no animosities.
We bomb all of Serbia's bridges
to stop all her atrocities.

(Just think about it.
If NATO had thought years ago
to bomb the bridges across the Thames
the war in Northern Ireland
could have been brought to a quicker end.)

(And when the war was over
and Serb troops had to retreat
the bridges they needed were clear for them.
Now that's planning that's hard to beat.)

We are NATO bombers.
We always aim to please.
It was an accident we hit an embassy.
Our apologies to the Chinese.

(The Chinese oppose NATO interference
in Serbia's private affairs.
We won't mention the Tibetan people
and the nasty little problem of theirs.)

We are incredible bomb droppers.
We drop our bombs with skill.
But in spite of incredible accuracy
a few of our bombs still kill.

"Unfortunately in any enterprise of this nature,"
the NATO spokesman said,
"there is always a small chance of *accidental* damage
leaving many people dead."

"The pilot dropped his bomb in good faith.
Regrettably he was not to know that minute
a train would cross the bridge
and most unfortunately, and we sincerely regret this, the
train had people in it."

Our aim on every mission
is what it has always been
to strike solely at the Serbian army
to debilitate their killing machine.

But the Serbs lined up hundreds of dummy tanks
which to us so high in the air
looked exactly like real ones
which we think was completely unfair.

So after eighty days of bombing
and all NATO's might deployed
because the Serbs used underhand tactics
there were just thirteen real tanks destroyed.

This is an humanitarian war
And with every raid
We've dropped half a million's worth
of humanitarian aid.

We are NATO bombers
and this was an humanitarian war.
We regret we smashed up Serbia
and broke international law.

Our weapons were very accurate.
Just occasionally things went wrong.
We regret 2000 civilians
have been killed by NATO bombs.

But good will come from evil.
There'll be work for years to come,
replacing those thousands of weapons
and creating an arms trade boom.

29 June - 15 July 99

The Pilot's Testament

I seek no glory.
I bear no anger.
I hate no man.

I do the unspeakable
on behalf of the ungrateful.
I bomb targets chosen by others.

I have surrendered my will
to a higher authority.
I trust the cause to be right
and the methods appropriate.
There is no place for questioning.
There can be no other way.

I do my duty.
You can rely on me.
I will not let you down.

Though my task may be dangerous,
neither fear nor doubt
will prevent me.

Consider me.
Physically and mentally
my ability is exceptional.
My judgement and reflexes
are trained to perfection.
I am chosen from the elite,
the very best.
Many accord me
great respect.

I possess power beyond imagination.
Like a god I roar through the heavens,
miraculous,
immaculate,
invulnerable,
supreme,
the earth beneath me,
the whole of creation
available to me,
awaiting
my quick shot
of death and destruction.

My victims are unaware of me.
I am unaware of my victims.

They go about their lives
not knowing only a few seconds remain.

We are arriving
at the appointed time and place.

At a touch I fix their fate.

Moments later,
in mid conversation,
a flash,
and they are gone.

I cannot pretend it was difficult.

Their will was done,
and I, merely an instrument of death.
I did my duty,
but I accept no guilt.

I come down to earth
as a man among men,
unmarked, unrecognised,
unremarkable, unnoticed:
I easily blend.

I am not available for comment.
I am not an item of news. The story is elsewhere.

I return to my family
as if nothing has happened.

15- 22 December 99

NATO Leaders After the War

The fact we saved the Kosovans
critics rarely mention.
All that destruction of Serbia was an unfortunate side effect
of our moral and pure intention.

7 July 99

Well Done, Serbian Soldiers *

Well done, you Serbian soldiers.
You survived the war grinning and free
and your convoys zoom back into Serbia
and all the world at its telly can see.

You did your bit for your country
with countless courageous attacks.
Ten thousand homes you faced without flinching
and destroyed them,
never fearing that they might fight back.

Your victims were ordinary people
just like your own relations and friends:
men, women, old folk, and children,
and their nightmare will not quickly end.
Did your mind not connect with these people?

And did you never consider the fact
that because you brought such terror and ruin,
your own people might never go back?

Weaker men might have felt sick at the suffering
or felt a touch of guilt or of shame,
but such things bring pleasure to heroes;
there's nothing more delightful than pain.

Well done, you Serbian soldiers.
Now Kosovo burns in its hell
and you can return safely to Serbia
with some wonderful stories to tell.

9 - 11 November 99

* It should not be assumed that the soldiers of the Serbian Army all shared in taking pleasure in their barbarous work. In any case most soldiers were conscripts. *Amnesty International* has reported that hundreds of young Serbian men evaded the draft or deserted. - In October 1999 *Amnesty* reported that at least several hundred soldiers were serving five year prison sentences in Yugoslavia for conscientious objection. "The number of such cases currently before the Federal Republic of Yugoslavia's military courts may be at least 23,000." Many Serb soldiers deserted in Kosovo.

Legacy

People with mutilated minds,
a paralysis of feeling,
locked in your culture of carnage and conflict,
after your tears and your trauma,
what message will you pass to your children?

11 July 99

Revenge

Hatred breeds hatred
and you have excelled in barbarism.
But how can you change
when you are overwhelmed by suffering?

Is it possible to suffer beyond belief,
to lose all you have worked for,
all you have loved,
and forgive?

Revenge calls out to you,
"Take me, and put an end
to all who gave you grief."

Revenge can only put an end
to hope.

10 July 99

Freedom Fighters

On Friday 23 July 1999, 14 Serb farmers were murdered, shot dead in Gracko, in Kosovo.

You are no heroes.
There are no heroes
with guns in their hands.
Was it clever or courageous
to ambush those farmers?

You are not freedom fighters.
Those men lie dead.
Where is your freedom?
Has your cause been advanced
by even the smallest fraction?

And what is your cause? -
Your cause is misery:
the allotment of death,
the bereavement of families
the creation of fear
the darkening of life,
the destruction of communities.

You are for nobody.
You help no-one.
You are against people,
against life,
against all that makes life worthwhile.

Freedom is advanced
by trust and co-operation,
perhaps courageously taking risks.

The only cause to fight for
is the betterment of humanity.

26 July 99

A *Human Rights Watch* report, quoted in *The Guardian* on 4 August, said that they had evidence of 30 cases of beating and kidnapping and the murder of 40 Serbs and 2 Gypsies in Kosovo since the arrival in mid-June of KFOR, the UN peace-keeping force.

The KFOR figure for murders in Kosovo to the end of October 1999 is 379.

To add to the general lawlessness it is widely reported that armed criminal gangs from Albania are operating throughout Kosovo.

Peace Terrorists

Rivers divide;
bridges unite.
Bridges unite people.
They unite communities.

But not in Mitrovica.
Here we have peace-keepers,
the arrogant French peace keepers,
peace-keepers who would keep us apart.

"This jeering mob
hurling rocks at us,
can it have peaceful intentions?
Soldiers, stand firm! Ils ne passeront pas!"

The peace agreement
promised a Kosovo
of integrated communities.
We, the young men of Albanian race

wish to integrate
with our Serbian compatriots
across the river.
That is our right, and we demand it.
Today we arrive in hundreds.
Those bastard peace-keepers
block our way - soldiers with guns,
a new tribe to hate,
laying barbed wire across the bridge!

What right have they
to guess our intentions,
to treat us like enemies
in our own country?

Bricks and bottles
for peace-keepers!
"Yah! Yah! Get out of our way!"
A hail of stones. "Let us pass!"

"This jeering mob
hurling rocks at us,
can it have peaceful intentions?
Soldiers, stand firm! Ils ne passeront pas!"

"Yah! Yah! You terrorist peace-keepers!
How dare you keep us
shut out of our own town!
We have our rights. We have our rights!

"Ha! Ha!" the Serbs across the river
call back. They taunt us.
"Neutral peace-keepers, we see which side
you support. But we have our rights."

"Let us get at them,
those jeering Serbs.
We have suffered at their hands
beyond endurance. We shall endure no more.
We shall reach them,
the Serbs. We shall teach them.
We shall deliver our message.
They will know the strength of our anger,
created by them,
a torrent of anger against their behaviour,

a river in flood that will not be halted.
This time it is not we who will be swept away."

10 August 99

Problems in Mitrovica

The problems in Mitrovica highlight the general peace-keeping problems faced by the international peace-keeping forces. Mitrovica is a town in northern Kosovo with a large Serbian population. Many Albanian Kosovars believe Mitrovica and other Serbian strongholds harbour Serbian para-militaries and war criminals. They fear that the industrially more wealthy northern edge of Kosovo may be seized back by Serbian troops, leaving the Albanians with an impoverished Kosovo.

Serbian troops have been seen gathering on the border. There has been an influx into Mitrovica and the surrounding area of "a surprising number of well-built, very short-haired, young Serbian men." Many Serbians remain well armed.

Rockets were fired over the river from the Albanian south into the predominantly Serbian north of the town on 10 August. Serbians in the north have since made revenge attacks on Albanians.

The peace-keepers have taken enormous trouble to cope with the intense inter-ethnic hostility. They have registered many people believed to be at risk, set up emergency telephone lines, reinforced doors of homes, lain in wait for attackers, and in some cases provided 24-hour guard. The scale of the hostility is so great that wholly successful peace-keeping is impossible, and when they fail to protect a victim they suffer blame as if they were the cause of the crime. Albanians in Mitrovica actually did accuse the French peace-keepers of being terrorists.

Backward Vision

Sadly I see your future:

supervised political arrangements
finely tuned,
perfectly balanced,
fair,
but, introduce your politicians
and the will isn't there.
They have problems with fixed mindsets,
old animosities
transparently disguised.
Every move is guarded.
They bicker, and are bloodyminded.

The problems you face are vast,
but you can't step into the future
because you are rooted in the past.

15 August 99

All Wars

All wars
are racist wars
fought against the evil them
by the self-righteous us.

13 June 99

Mental Block

Nervous armed gangs
(of explosive temperament and with short fuses)
terrify people,
but can't understand
what all the fuss is.

Politicians
(of good intentions, and favouring peace)
advise them quietly
to give up weapons.
Shock! Horror! Alarm!

How could we walk
down the street
without our arms?
We would feel naked,
be a laughing stock.

Emotional
problems include compulsive urges
to set off explosions,
and some men suffer from in-growing machine-guns.

Attempts at
surgical removal
have precipitated shock;
and, sadly,
therapy and medication
have proved ineffective
against a permanent mental block.

15 July - 17 August 99

Disarming the KLA

An agreement was signed on 21 June between KFOR and the Kosovo Provisional Government demobilising and demilitarising the KLA. Weapons were to be handed in by 21 September.

A huge gesture was made. Almost 10,000 small arms were handed in, plus 5.5 million rounds of ammunition and several hundred mortars, machine guns and anti-tank weapons.

Agim Ceku, former military leader of the KLA, claimed that attacks on aged civilians were not the work of the KLA. The leadership forbade such behaviour. Unfortunately anyone could easily buy KLA uniforms and some criminals were doing this.

It is reckoned that thousands of former KLA fighters still retain weapons they bought with their own money - small arms and Kalashnikovs, and that weapons are still pouring over the Albanian border into Kosovo.

History

History is taught
to foster racial illusions.
Who but the British
believe in the moral superiority
of the British?

Badges to Die for

Men hide behind badges of race, creed and class
and forget their identity
as fellow members of the human race.
For such symbols they kill and die.

13 June 99

There Will Be No Peace

There will be no peace:

till attitudes change;
till self-interest is seen as part of common interest;
till old wrongs, old scores, old mistakes
    are deleted from the account;
till the aim becomes co-operation and mutual benefit
    rather than revenge or seizing maximum personal
    or group gain;
till justice and equality before the law
    become the basis of government;
till basic freedoms exist;
till leaders - political, religious, educational - and
    the police and media
    wholeheartedly embrace the concepts
    of justice, equality, freedom, tolerance, and
    reconciliation
    as a basis for renewal;
till parents teach their children new ways to think
    about people.

There will be no peace:
till enemies become fellow human beings.

22 July 99

A Just War

You killed our families.
So we will kill yours.
This is just a war,
they said.
And we will go on killing
just until everyone is dead.

14 June 99

A Violent or a Peaceful World - Making or Breaking

The promoters of narrow patriotism, nationalism and racism suffer from a moral short-sightedness which leads to the kind of misery and horror we have witnessed in Yugoslavia in the last ten years of the twentieth century. Not only Serbs and Kosovo Albanians acted on racist motives, but NATO nations, too. Leaders who base action on racist attitudes lack a vision of the world appropriate to the needs of their people and the world as a whole.

All races are in a minority. All need the support and co-operation of others. All could make better use of their time and talent if they directed their energies to co-operative problem solving, rather than the harassment and extermination of others they have picked on to blame for their troubles.

The fate of the people of the world is linked. We prosper or die together. We have a choice.

Making or Breaking

We inherit the world,
the whole of history,
our place on earth,
our place in time,
our fortune, good or bad,
pure chance.

Now,
in one picture,
we see our entire planet:
one world,
one race,
one future,
bound together for the first time.
Ours for the breaking
or making.

12 December 99

Main Sources of Information

BBC radio and television news, documentaries and web site; Channel 4 documentary, *The Valley*; web sites of NATO, MOD, OSCE, UNHCR, UN, Amnesty international, International Crisis Group, The Transnational Organisation, Kosova Press, Serbian Government.
The Balkans 1804-1999 by Misha Glenny, Granta Books, 1999. *Kosovo - How Myths and Truths Started a War* by Julie Mertus, University of California Press, 1999. *Kosovo - A Short History* by Noel Malcolm, Papermac, 1998. *Fighting for Peace* by Michael Rose, Warner Books, 1998.

Also published by Saxon Books

Minds at War

The Poetry and Experience of the First World War

Edited by David Roberts

410 pages 9x6" Paperback Illustrated Third Printing

ISBN 0 952 8969 0 7 £13-99 (UK)

Minds at War is the largest anthology of poetry of the First World War and has a wealth of background information. It has 50 per cent more poems than the Penguin Anthology of First World War Poetry.

The poetry

- The selection concentrates on the classic poems by the greatest poets of the war
- Women poets are exceptionally well represented
- There are examples of the once hugely popular poems which were written as propaganda.

Important background

Historical and biographical background material, extracts from diaries, personal letters and autobiographies of poets illuminate the poetry. The comments of generals, pundits, politicians, newspapers and ordinary people help to provide the necessary context and deepen our appreciation.

Enthusiastic comments

"Read this compelling book" - Rex Andrews in *The Friend*.
"Absolutely wonderful" - Pat Davidson, Poetry Buyer, Waterstones, Worcester.
"Remarkable . . . absorbing . . . stimulating . . . Do buy it," - Ronald Mallone in *Day by Day*
We recommend *Minds at War* as a valuable resource for teachers, advanced students, libraries, and all who are interested in what people who were involved in the war thought about it.

Out in the Dark

Poetry of the First World War in Context and with Basic Notes

Edited by David Roberts

192 pages, 9x6" Paperback, Illustrated, Second Printing

ISBN 0 952 8969 1 5 £7-99 (UK)

For students and the general reader

This anthology, based on **Minds at War**, has been prepared for the general reader who requires less background information than there is in **Minds at War**, and for students, including GCSE and A level, who need to understand the contexts of poems.

Out in the Dark contains:

- the great classic poems of the First World War
- a wide range of popular verse, and propagandist verse
- a substantial selection of poems by women writers
- basic notes on almost all poems (140 in total)
- ample material for in-depth course work studies
- important historical and biographical information
- Comments of past and present day critics give starting points for considering "alternative interpretations" of many poems

Appreciating the poems

This anthology of war poetry, with its contextual material and strong illustrations will prove a stimulating and rewarding aid to appreciating the poetry and events of the First World War.

"The best war poetry anthology for students."

More information on www.saxonbooks.co.uk

KOSOVO WAR POETRY AND VERSE

with background notes

by David Roberts

The war that made Europeans feel guilty.
A personal response.

For three months in 1999 the attention of the world was focused on Serbia and Kosovo as the most powerful military alliance in the world bombed the poorest nation in Europe into submission. The extreme violence of that campaign, and of the behaviour of many Serbs and Kosovo Albanians before and since that war raises issues which concern all responsible people.

- In tough and uncompromising poems and satirical verse David Roberts explores the human suffering, the power of hatred, the propaganda, the moral arguments, and NATO's "humanitarian" bombing campaign.
- An introductory essay reveals something of the causes, development and consequences of the violence in Serbia and Kosovo.

David Roberts is the editor of two anthologies of First World War poetry.

Back cover: Serbian soldiers celebrate the burning of another Kosovo Albanian home. (See *Have a Nice Day*.)

ISBN 0 952 8969 2 3 Saxon Books £4-99 (UK)